GROSS AND GHASTLY

HUMAN BODY

BY KEV PAYNE

DK

CONTENTS

WHAT'S INSIDE?

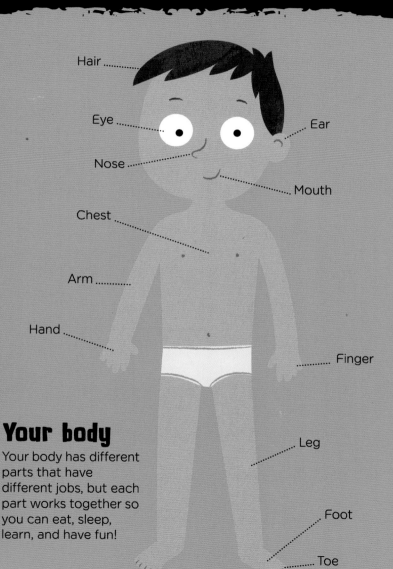

Hair

Eye

Nose

Ear

Mouth

Chest

Arm

Hand

Finger

Leg

Foot

Toe

Your body

Your body has different parts that have different jobs, but each part works together so you can eat, sleep, learn, and have fun!

Puking, pooping, sweating, and peeing—inside our bodies there are systems that help keep things running smoothly. If you peel back the skin you can see everything that lies underneath!

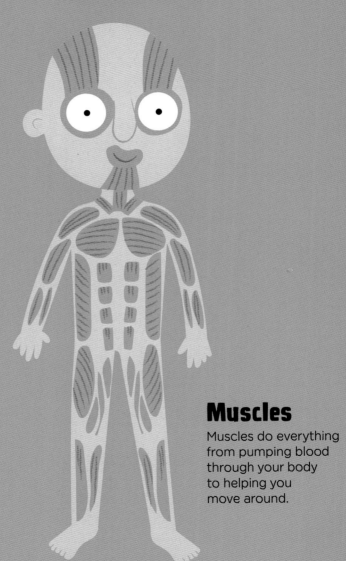

Muscles

Muscles do everything from pumping blood through your body to helping you move around.

BITS AND BONES!

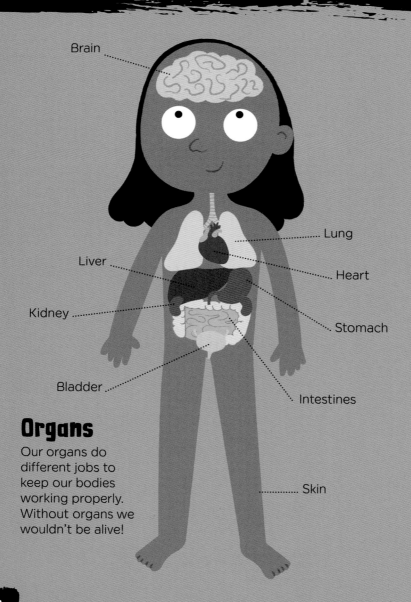

Brain

Lung

Liver

Heart

Kidney

Stomach

Bladder

Intestines

Organs

Our organs do different jobs to keep our bodies working properly. Without organs we wouldn't be alive!

Skin

Beneath the muscles there's a whole world of organs to discover. And if you keep going you'll find your skeleton.

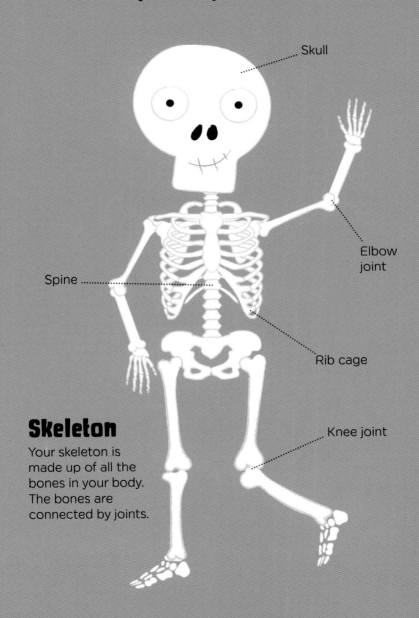

Skull

Elbow joint

Spine

Rib cage

Knee joint

Skeleton

Your skeleton is made up of all the bones in your body. The bones are connected by joints.

SUPER POOP!

Poop is the waste that remains after you've digested your food and absorbed the nutrients into your body. The texture, smell, and look of your poop changes due to your diet and lifestyle. Here, you can find out a lot of facts about poop.

What is thought to be the world's largest fossilized human poop was found by archaeologists in 1972. It measures 8 inches (20 centimeters) long!

Why is poop brown?

Poop starts off a greeny-yellow color but changes as it travels through your body to become brown. Depending on what you eat and drink, and how healthy you are, sometimes your poop can be other colors, such as green, yellow, red, white, or black.

Staying afloat

"Floaters" are poops that refuse to be flushed and instead float on the surface of the water in the toilet. If you eat something that gives you extra gas, it can cause the poop to rise to the surface.

Poop paint

Famous artist, Pablo Picasso, is said to have used some of his daughter's poop in one of his paintings. He used it to paint an apple.

POWERFUL PEE

Pee, piddle, and tinkle—whatever the name, it's all a mixture of water, salts, and chemicals. Made in the kidneys and stored in the bladder, pee removes unwanted substances from your blood. Let's dive into an ocean of facts all about pee!

Gotta go

Most people pee between six and eight times a day. If you're drinking a lot of fluids, however, or on certain medications, then it can be more. The amount of pee produced by a person each day is around 6 cups (1.5 liters)—enough to fill a bathtub every month!

Drop of color

The color and smell of your pee can depend on a number of factors, including what you've eaten, how much you've had to drink, and your general health. The color is usually pale yellow, but pee can also be green, orange, or blue. Eating beets can even turn your pee pink!

Come on, I gotta charge my phone!

Researchers have found ways of turning pee into electricity. At the moment it can be used to power smartphones or lighting, but a research team are developing ways of using it to power an electric car.

Piddling pool

Chlorine is a chemical put into swimming pools to help protect the water from germs, and most people can recognize its smell. The smell, however, actually comes from the chemical reaction of the chlorine with the oils, sweat, and pee from the people in the pool.

DISASTROUS DISEASES

Diseases stop parts of the body from functioning properly. Hundreds of diseases exist, some of which can be treated with medication. Find out more about some of the more disastrous diseases that nature has made.

Flesh-eating disease

Necrotizing fasciitis is a very rare, dangerous infection that can damage and destroy skin, fat, and tissue very quickly. It spreads rapidly and is life threatening. It can be treated with antibiotics if caught early but sometimes limbs are amputated to save a person's life.

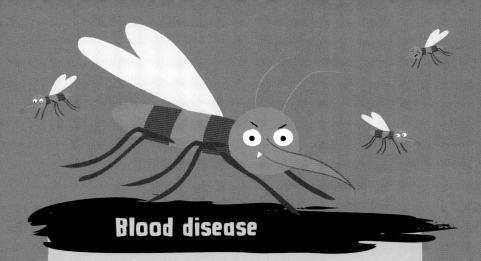

Blood disease

Malaria is an infectious disease mostly caused by mosquitoes who spread it when they bite people. Malaria can be mild in some people and more serious in others. Getting the right treatment can help cure the disease but it still accounts for 500,000 deaths a year worldwide.

Guinea worm disease

Guinea worm disease is caused by drinking water that contains guinea worm larvae. The eggs are spread around by fleas. There are no initial symptoms but, after a year, victims may develop a fever and swelling. The worms then pop out through painful blisters on the skin.

DISGUSTING DIGESTION

Digestion is how our bodies break down food and liquid so we get nutrients and energy. The digestive system runs all the way from our mouths to our bottoms. So whether you eat carrots or chocolate, it's all going to end up in the same place!

Strong stuff

The acid in our stomach has to be superstrong to break down all the food we shove into our mouths! Acids are measured using pH levels that range from 0 to 14, with 0 being the strongest. Our stomach acids usually range from 1 to 3—powerful enough to destroy metal.

Since our stomach lining is constantly battered by acids, our bodies make a new lining every few days. It is made of mucus, similar to the stuff that drips from our noses!

Long stretch

Our intestines (the tubes that go from our stomachs to our bottoms) are all packed neatly into our bodies. If we were to stretch them out in a straight line, they would reach nearly 30 feet (around 9 meters). That's about the same length as a small bus!

Toilet break

The time it takes to digest your food depends on what you have eaten. Once the food has been crushed and swallowed, it can take between two and five days before you see it again in your poop.

FUNKY FEET

Stinky and sweaty—feet have a tough job trying to support our entire bodies. They hold a quarter of all the bones in our body and, like our fingerprints, our toe prints are unique to us, too.

Say cheese!

Sometimes the expression "cheesy feet" is used in relation to some of the stinky gunk that appears on your feet. In Ireland in 2013, an exhibition featured real cheese made using the bacteria found between people's toes.

Fat Feet

A baby's feet are much more flexible than an adult's, because the foot bones haven't yet developed. Feet continue growing until your teenage years. Babies' feet are adorable because of the fat pad they have in place of the arch of the foot—it makes them look chubby and cute. The fat pad disappears once the foot muscles start to develop.

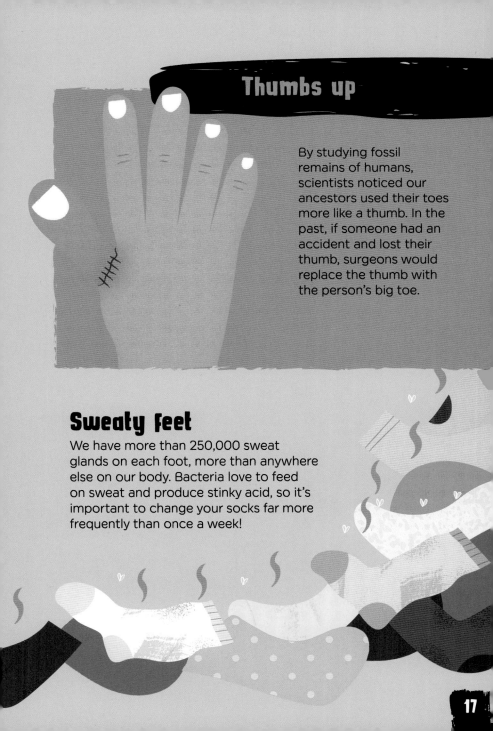

Thumbs up

By studying fossil remains of humans, scientists noticed our ancestors used their toes more like a thumb. In the past, if someone had an accident and lost their thumb, surgeons would replace the thumb with the person's big toe.

Sweaty feet

We have more than 250,000 sweat glands on each foot, more than anywhere else on our body. Bacteria love to feed on sweat and produce stinky acid, so it's important to change your socks far more frequently than once a week!

SWEAT IT OUT

Sweat is the body's way of getting rid of moisture when trying to cool us down. When we are too hot, the sweat evaporates off our skin, helping to lower our temperature. It is mainly made up of water but also contains salt and other chemicals.

Buzz off!

Sweat bees are attracted to human sweat and will even drink it. The natural reaction may be to swat the bees away, but this may cause them to sting. If you cry, then the bees may drink your tears, too!

Stinky sweat

By itself, sweat does not smell, but a smell is produced when it interacts with the bacteria that are living on our skin. Sweat glands are found all over the body, even on the eyelids.

The amount you sweat depends on a number of factors, such as your age, health, and if you are being active or not. During an hour of exercise, people sweat out about 2 cups (0.5 liters) but it can even be as much as 3.2 quarts (3 liters).

Veggies rule!

Sweat samples were collected from people who were vegetarians and compared to those who ate meat. People were asked to sniff the sweat and decide which smelled better. Results showed that the vegetarian sweat was much more appealing.

Sweating can leave your body feeling dehydrated, so it's important to make sure you drink plenty of water.

VILE VOMIT

Vomiting is the body's way of trying to eject something that it sees as harmful or irritating in the body. It can be a normal and helpful process although an unpleasant one. There are many causes of vomiting, including food poisoning, germs, or even going on a fast roller coaster!

Barf time

Vomit is made up of half-digested food, chemicals, and stomach juices that get mixed together. People often wonder why there are chunks of carrot in their vomit, even if they haven't eaten them. Scientists believe that they are bits of stomach lining.

That's sick!

White, yellow, green, or orange—the color of your vomit can depend on a number of factors, including what you've eaten, and whether you have an illness—and what illness it is. Clear vomit usually occurs after you've been sick several times and have no more food in your stomach.

Sick justice

Police will study vomit if it has been left at a crime scene because it may contain useful information about what has happened, or who may be responsible. DNA can be extracted from the vomit, and matched to the criminal.

Throw up and away!

Projectile vomiting is when a person is sick in short bursts, with a lot of force. Experiments have shown that droplets of projectile vomit can be found more than 23 feet (7 meters) away from the person throwing up—that's as far as the length of a delivery van!

BRILLIANT BOOGERS

Boogers, snot, mucus—it's all the same thing and can be found hanging in, or out of, your nose. Brilliant boogers are everywhere!

Picky eaters

Some people have the really disgusting habit of eating their boogers. It's not advisable! Snot helps trap harmful bacteria and viruses that may otherwise have entered the body, so eating it is not a great idea.

Mucus menu

Eating certain foods can increase or decrease your production of snot. Butter, ice cream, cheese, and eggs can all lead to an increase in mucus production. But pineapple, fish, and chili can work the opposite way.

Rainbow snot

Snot isn't always green. Black snot appears if you've been inhaling a lot of soot or dust, yellow can be a sign of fighting an infection, and there is even a type of bacteria that turns your snot blue!

Snot money

In 2008, after appearing on a talk show where she blew her nose, actress Scarlett Johansson auctioned off the used tissue for charity. The winning bidder paid more than $5,000 to take home the prize.

You'll need to give me $5,000 to even touch that!

BEASTLY BACTERIA

Bacteria can be both helpful and harmful to our bodies. For instance, good bacteria can help us digest our food, but bad bacteria can give us a stomachache. Bacteria are microorganisms, which means you need a microscope to see them.

Big numbers

Our mouths are home to as many as six billion bacteria—that's almost the same number as the amount of people on Earth. All bacteria go through a cycle of being born, feeding, breeding, and dying.

The human cells are winning!

Poop it out

Bacteria live on us and in us in enormous amounts. The average person has about the same number of human cells and bacterial cells. We can lose up to a third of our bacteria when we poop.

Button up!

In 2011, during a study on bacteria living in belly buttons, researchers made some surprising discoveries. They found some unusual bacteria on the participants, including bacteria from Japanese soil on a man who had never been to Japan, and someone who was carrying bacteria from the polar ice caps!

I have no idea how that got there.

Looking flushed

There is a lot of harmful bacteria in our poop. It's best to flush the toilet with the lid down, otherwise you could spread an invisible cloud of bad bacteria up into the air, as high as 15 feet (4.6 meters). That's nearly as tall as a giraffe! The bacteria can survive for a long time on counters, towels, and even your toothbrush.

IT'S THE PITS

Our armpits are underneath the upper arm, near the shoulder, and are among the warmest places on our bodies. They contain a lot of sweat glands.

Makes scents

Smelly armpits are caused by bacteria feeding off sweat. If the smell becomes a really bad problem, it's possible for doctors to take bacteria from someone who doesn't smell as bad and transfer it to the armpits of someone that does.

Armpit

No show

In 2013, seven-year-old Erich Henze from Detroit in the US, made the news after he was banned from performing in his school talent show. His "talent" was making fart noises with his armpits, legs, neck, and ears.

Unique scent

You can choose to mask the smell of sweat by using deodorants. While the most popular types are a mixture of oils, flowers, and herbs there are also a range of unique scents including bacon and pizza!

If we are stressed, our armpits will sweat out 30 times more sweat than if we are resting.

Mmm, bacon!

Not to be sniffed at

Looking for a new career? Then a job as an armpit sniffer might be the one for you! Armpit sniffers work for deodorant companies, spending their days sniffing up to 60 armpits an hour to see which products will be good for the market.

WILD WORLD RECORDS

The human body is capable of incredible things, but some people like to push it to the extreme. There are some really wild world records out there!

Shave it for later

Ram Singh Chauhan from India is the proud owner of the world's longest mustache. The mustache measures more than 14 feet (4.29 meters), that's about as long as an elephant! Chauhan has been growing his mustache for more than 40 years.

Burptastic!

Paul Hunn, also known as "The Burper King," holds the record for the loudest burp by a male. With a burp registered at 109.9 decibels, it is louder than a vacuum cleaner, electric drill, and even a motorcycle. Hunn credits his ability to his love of soda.

Ilker Yilmaz from Turkey holds the long-distance record for squirting milk from his eye. For the record attempt, Yilmaz snorted the milk up into his nose before shooting it a whopping 9 feet 2 inches (279.5 centimeters) from his left eye. That's the length of three shopping carts end to end!

Can't be licked!

Nick "The Lick" Stoeberl from California, US, has the world's longest male tongue at 3.9 inches (10.1 centimeters) long. The average tongue is 3.3 inches (8.5 centimeters). In 2016, he appeared on the TV show *America's Got Talent* where he painted a picture using his enormous tongue as a brush.

SCABBY SCABS

It is pretty certain you have seen a scab or two on your body at some point. Scabs appear on our skin after a cut or a scrape. The crusty patches are the body's way of protecting itself from germs, while new skin forms underneath.

Food for thought

Scabs usually fall off after a week or two. Some people, however, may be tempted to pick, or even eat their scabs. This can make the wound bleed again, or leave a scar. Eating a scab may give you some protein, but you'll swallow a lot of germs and dirt, too.

Crust creator

As soon as skin has been damaged, special blood cells called platelets rush to the scene of the injury and stick together. The platelets work to create a scab that hardens as it dries out.

Ooze

Sometimes a yellow crust can appear at the edges of a scab. This is a sign that pus, a fluid your body creates when fighting off infection, is building up underneath it. Sometimes cracks will appear in the scab, and the pus will ooze out.

Pus is a mixture of dead blood cells, living or dead bacteria, and tissue.

OH BABY!

Cute and cuddly, or noisy and stinky? Babies are gross, just like the rest of us! Babies need special care and lots of cuddling—even when they have a stinky diaper. Find out some incredible facts about those bouncy, brilliant, burping babies!

Bony baby!

Babies have more bones than adults, around 300 in total. The bones are mostly made of cartilage, a rubbery, flexible material. They fuse together and harden as the baby grows, to become the 206 bones a person will have as an adult.

Cutie pie

Ever wonder why a baby looks so cute with their big eyes? That's because a baby's eyes are nearly as big as an adult's! The color of the eyes can change, too, normally at around six months, but even as old as three years.

Did you know?
Babies are born
with the ability
to swim!

First plops

Within the first 24 to 48 hours of
being born, babies will have their first
poop, which is thick, and a bit like tar.
After about three days, their poop will
change color to light-brown, yellow,
or even green with the consistency
of peanut butter.

Hidden treasure

When exploring the world
and their own bodies,
babies and toddlers often
put objects into their ears
or noses. Doctors have to
remove items such as peas,
marbles, buttons, and beads.
Medical staff in China discovered
one child with a dandelion growing
out of their ear!

FOUL FARTS

Farts are the process of expelling gas through the bottom. Some may be silent, some may be noisy, but one thing is for sure... they all come out of the same place!

What is in a fart?

Most of a fart does not smell and is made up of 99 percent odorless gases. The final 1 percent contains different compounds that include sulfur and this is what causes the stink.

Pass the gas

On average, we fart about 14 times a day. The amount of gas we produce each day is around 2 cups (0.5 liters), enough to fill a balloon.

I filled it all by myself!

Farty food

Some foods *do* make you more farty and these include lentils, onions, cabbage, brussels sprouts, and cauliflower. To make your farts less smelly, researchers have found that bananas, potatoes, and cereals can help to reduce the odor. There is even an inventor in France who claims he has made a pill that makes your farts smell like chocolate!

Famous farts

Some people fart for a living. These include Mr. Methane from the UK, who farts along to music; Le Petomane from France, who could blow out candles with his farts; and Roland the Farter, a 12th-century jester who would entertain King Henry II by farting for him every Christmas.

BEAUTIFUL BLOOD

Blood is made up of plasma, white blood cells, red blood cells, and platelets. Every time our hearts beat, blood is pumped through our bodies. The blood carries nutrients and oxygen to our cells before returning to the heart.

Around the world

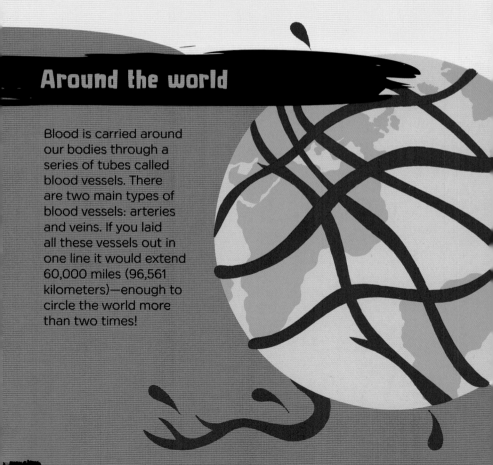

Blood is carried around our bodies through a series of tubes called blood vessels. There are two main types of blood vessels: arteries and veins. If you laid all these vessels out in one line it would extend 60,000 miles (96,561 kilometers)—enough to circle the world more than two times!

Blood red... and gold?

The red color of our blood comes from a protein called hemoglobin which picks up oxygen in the lungs. Our blood also contains iron and a yellow-colored plasma which is sometimes known as liquid gold!

Beat it

The average resting heartbeat of an adult is between 60 and 100 beats per minute but this depends on your age and fitness. By comparison, a mouse's heart beats over 500 beats per minute, while an elephant is just 30 beats per minute. This might increase if the elephant saw the mouse scurrying around its feet!

MONSTROUS MEDICINE

Medicines help people fight illness or stop them from getting sick in the first place. Doctors think very carefully when choosing medicines to help sick people. New medicines are invented all the time, and doctors and scientists are always finding new ways of helping us keep healthy.

Mystery illness

When choosing a medicine, doctors have to consider what may be the cause of the illness. In China, a 37-year-old man went to the hospital with a severe cough and breathing problems. Doctors realized that the infection had been caused by the man sniffing his dirty, fungus-filled socks at the end of each day!

Bad taste

The ingredients that are used to help a medicine do its job don't always taste that good. Children often don't like medicine because the flavors are typically salty and bitter, and children's taste buds are more sensitive to these.

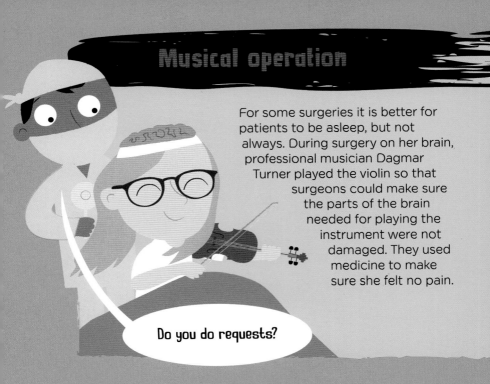

For some surgeries it is better for patients to be asleep, but not always. During surgery on her brain, professional musician Dagmar Turner played the violin so that surgeons could make sure the parts of the brain needed for playing the instrument were not damaged. They used medicine to make sure she felt no pain.

Do you do requests?

Mold maker

Penicillin is an antibiotic medicine that is used to treat a range of infections. It was discovered by accident in 1928 by Alexander Fleming who came back to his lab after a vacation and found that mold was killing some of the bacteria he had been growing. Before it was given the name penicillin in 1929 it was known as "mold juice."

Mmm, juicy!

MORE POOP!

The subject of poop is endlessly interesting. Everyone does it! And we just can't stop talking about it.

Long shot

It is estimated that the longest poop was 26 feet long (7.92 meters) long. The woman who produced the mammoth stool ate a very high-fiber diet and didn't go to the bathroom for a week beforehand.

Hot stuff

Spicy foods can make your bottom feel like it is on fire when you go to the bathroom. The hole in your bottom is lined with sensitive cells, similar to those in your mouth, so it can be just as hot on the way out as it was on the way in.

Fire starter

In Kenya, a company uses compressed blocks of human poop as an alternative to charcoal and firewood. Using human waste helps save trees from being cut down. The poop goes through a processthat makes the fuel odorless— thank goodness.

Surprise!

If you've ever eaten corn, you may have noticed how it appears again in your poop. This is because the outer layer of corn is made of cellulose, which our bodies are unable to break down. However, we can digest the inner part of the corn so what we see is just the shell.

BATTERED BONES

As adults, we have 206 bones in our body. From helping us move to protecting vital organs, bones help us perform everyday activities. Without bones we wouldn't have much shape and we wouldn't be able to walk, run, or pick up this book to read all the ghastly facts!

Blood factory

Although they seem strong and hard, bones are actually hollow tubes filled with a spongy tissue called bone marrow. This bone marrow is also responsible for making our blood! It produces all kinds of blood cells that our bodies need and makes billions of them a day!

A new you

As adults, our bodies remove old pieces of bone every year which are replaced with fresh bone tissue. After about 10 years we have a brand new skeleton!

Funny fact

If you've ever bumped it, you may well agree that the funny bone is not funny at all. It's also not even a bone! The tingly feeling we get near our elbow is due to a nerve in our arm that shoots down to our fingertips.

Record breaker

Stuntman Evel Knievel holds the record for most broken bones over the course of a career. Using his motorcycle, Knievel regularly jumped over cars, buses, rattlesnakes, and lions—but sometimes he crashed, leading to a total of 433 broken bones over a number of years. Once he broke both arms rehearsing a jump over a tank full of sharks!

QUEASY QUESTIONS

Who? What? Where? When? Why? How? Our world is filled with questions, and here are the answers to some of the disgusting questions that may be on the tip of your tongue!

Why does vomit burn my throat when I throw up?

The acids in our digestive system help us break down and digest our food. When we throw up, the bitter, sour taste that is left in our mouths is from these acids.

Can you make a candle out of ear wax?

No. Normal candles are made with paraffin or beeswax that burns slowly. Ear wax burns quickly and with a crackling sound. The dead skin cells, hair, and fatty acids mean it won't melt or burn consistently enough for a candle.

Why don't I mind the smell of my own farts?

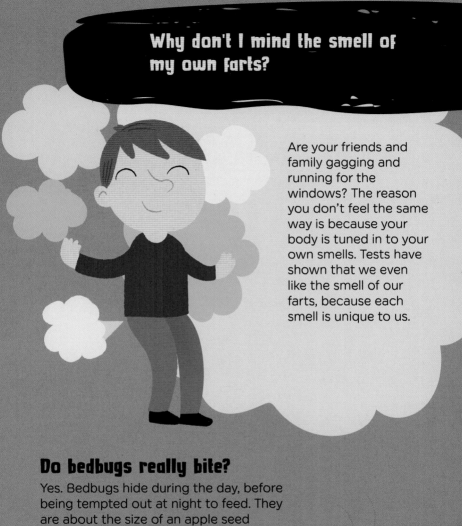

Are your friends and family gagging and running for the windows? The reason you don't feel the same way is because your body is tuned in to your own smells. Tests have shown that we even like the smell of our farts, because each smell is unique to us.

Do bedbugs really bite?

Yes. Bedbugs hide during the day, before being tempted out at night to feed. They are about the size of an apple seed and have flat bodies before they start a meal. They can suck up to seven times their own body weight in blood which leaves them much fatter than when they started feeding.

SILLY SENSES

Our senses help us understand the outside world. There are five main senses, called the "special senses," but scientists believe we may have as many as 21! The extra senses include a sense of space and balance. Close your eyes and swing your arms around. You will sense where your arms are.

Taste

The average person has around 10,000 taste buds. If you stick out your tongue you can see them as little bumps. Taste buds help us taste the five tastes—salty, bitter, sour, sweet, and umami, which is how savory something is.

Sight

We actually "see" things upside down. The eye sends messages to the brain, which turns the picture the right way up. It is thought that newborn babies see things upside down until the brain learns to flip everything the right way.

Touch

Our sense of touch helps us react quickly to different situations. If we stand on a sharp object, we need our sense of touch to act quickly. These messages can go from the foot to the brain at 100 miles (160 kilometers) per hour!

Smell

What is your favorite smell? Do you know that you can actually smell if someone's happy? Researchers have found that we give off scent signals to show a range of emotions, including joy, disgust, and fear.

You smell... annoyed?

Hearing

Technology company Microsoft has built the "quietest place on Earth." It is a special chamber where the noise level has been measured at just over -20 decibels. To compare, a whisper is 30 decibels, and our breathing is around an ear-deafening 10 decibels.

MAGNIFICENT MUSCLES

There are more than 600 muscles in our bodies. These muscles help us keep our shape, allow us to move, and help us lift heavy objects. We can control a lot of our muscles, but some work without us knowing about it at all—like the heart!

Beat it!

The heart is an organ made out of muscle and is about the size of your fist. Every day, it beats over 100,000 times and pumps about 1540 gallons (7,000 liters) of blood around your body. The heart never has a day off and works even when we're asleep.

Super facers!

We have 43 muscles in our face that we use to create thousands of facial expressions. Scientists study people called "super facers," who are able to control each of the 43 muscles in their face individually.

Are you hungry? Angry? Tired?

Work it out

Exercise can help build and improve a range of muscles— including those that help you poop. One suggested workout for strengthening your bottom involves tensing the muscles you use to stop yourself from farting.

I can't hold it much longer!

Super!

Superhuman strength is a short burst of superstrength that humans can possess if they are faced with a near-death situation. There are plenty of stories of superhuman strength, including Tom Boyle from the US, who lifted a car to release a trapped cyclist, and Lydia Angyiou from Canada who fought off a polar bear that was about to attack her children.

49

EYE OPENERS!

Our eyes act like cameras, taking in images of the world around us and sending them to the brain to be processed and understood. There are more than two million moving parts in each eye, which can distinguish between millions of colors and shapes. Feast your eyes on some of these foul eye facts.

Babies may cry a lot but they do not actually start producing tears until they are around two weeks old!

Popping out

Kim Goodman, from the US, is famous for being able to pop her eyeballs out of their sockets. She holds the record for the farthest eyeball pop and is able to extend her eyes by 0.5 inches (12 millimeters). Kim first discovered her unique talent when she was accidentally hit in the eye at a Halloween party.

Eye watering

Do you cry when you cut an onion? It's because of the gas that is released. The gas reacts with chemicals in your eyes to produce an acid. The brain sends a message to the tear glands telling them to produce flowing tears to wash the acid away.

I'm too young to fry!

Lost lenses

During an eye operation on a 67-year-old woman in the UK, doctors were surprised to find a large, light-blue mass behind her right eye. They discovered that the lump was made up of 17 contact lenses that had gelled together with mucus. Another 10 loose lenses were discovered, meaning she'd lost a total of 27 lenses inside her eye.

ACHOO!

Sneezing is an involuntary action, which means it is something our body does automatically. Tiny hairs in our nose get tickled and send a message to the brain to let the sneezing begin—achoo!

Sneeze snooze

Sneezing is a reaction to the nose being irritated by something, like dirt, germs, or allergies, but some people also sneeze if they look at the sun. You don't sneeze in your sleep because the sneeze receptors in your brain are asleep, too.

Speedy snot

When we sneeze, the spray comes out of our mouths, not our noses, and can reach speeds of 100 miles (160 kilometers) per hour. That's faster than any car should go on a highway! Droplets from our sneezes can travel as far as 26 feet (8 meters), nearly as long as a city bus!

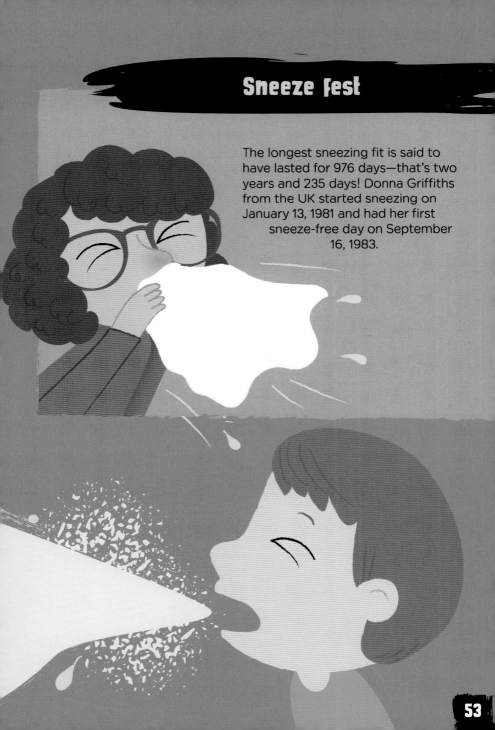

Sneeze Fest

The longest sneezing fit is said to have lasted for 976 days—that's two years and 235 days! Donna Griffiths from the UK started sneezing on January 13, 1981 and had her first sneeze-free day on September 16, 1983.

UPS AND DOWNS

As soon as we're born we sense emotions. Our feelings can be caused by many things, including where we are or who we're with. Scientists believe we may be able to experience as many as 27 different emotions, including joy, excitement, sadness, and disgust. So how does that make you feel?

Happy days

Matthieu Ricard, a monk, has been called "The World's Happiest Man." During a 12-year brain study, scientists connected sensors to his head and found that the part of his brain capable of feeling happiness was abnormally large.

Eww!

In the 1990s, Dr. Valerie Curtis did a study about disgust to find out what really makes people go "Eww!" She surveyed people from all over the world and found that there were some things that a lot of people found disgusting. The lengthy list included poop, toenail clippings, rotting meat, flies, blood, and pus.

Little learners

Young children develop their sense of disgust around the ages of two and three. Before then, they may reject things that taste bad but will not be disgusted by it. Studies have shown that young children learn disgust from the way their parents react.

Smash!

Everybody gets angry. You may stomp your feet or slam your door, but some people choose to use destruction therapy to get out their anger. This is when people visit special "rage rooms" and smash up old TVs, computers, and even cars. Of course, there are other ways of dealing with anger that don't involve smashing things to pieces!

SPIT BY SPIT

Drool, spit, spittle, slobber—saliva is known by many different names. It helps us swallow food, protects our teeth, and aids digestion. We produce less while sleeping and more while eating— or looking at a delicious piece of pizza!

How productive

You produce between 2 and 6 cups (0.5 and 1.5 liters) of drool a day, most of which is swallowed and reabsorbed. Over the course of your lifetime, you'll produce enough saliva to fill more than 50 bathtubs.

Long spit

There are a number of spitting competitions all over the world, where different things are spit over the longest distance possible. These include cherry pits, champagne corks, and even dried crickets and dung.

Scary saliva

You make less spit when you're scared. Your flow of saliva is controlled by the nervous system, and this will slow down production if you're in a "fight or flight" situation. So if you're eating salty popcorn when you're watching a scary movie, you might want to have something to drink handy.

Saliva interacts with food and makes you more sensitive to its flavor.

TIME TO GO!

One page of pee facts not enough for you? Let's learn even more about this liquid that's mostly water and is produced by every human on Earth!

Liquid gold

Pee has been used as an addition to compost due to the extra nitrogen and minerals it can add to soil. But have you ever seen a "straw bale urinal"? This is where straw bales are placed beside compost heaps to be peed on at festivals—they can then be used in the compost.

Taste test

In the past, doctors would diagnose medical conditions by tasting a patient's pee. They would use urine flavor charts, that described the taste, smell, and color of urine in relation to the condition. If the pee tasted sweet, for example, it could be a sign of diabetes.

Settle down

This could be where they used to pee!

You think?!

TOILET

Scientists have been able to identify when and where our ancestors settled down by looking at their 10,000-year-old pee. Studies of an ancient village in Turkey discovered salty deposits, that can be found in urine, which showed that humans chose to settle there.

Jellyfish joke

There's a long-held belief that peeing on a jellyfish sting helps reduce the pain, but numerous studies have shown that this is not the case. In fact, it may even trigger the jellyfish stings to release more venom. Still, you'd probably give the rest of the beach animals a good giggle!

PESKY PARASITES

Parasites are living organisms that feed off "hosts"—us—by living on our skin or inside our bodies. Some parasites spread disease, some cause pain, and some exist without us even knowing that they are there.

Wiggle room

Pinworms are tiny, thin worms that are white in color, and less than 0.5 inches (1.5 centimeters) in length. They get into our bodies when we accidentally swallow their eggs. Pinworms can have no symptoms, but some people may experience a lack of sleep, and have an itchy butt. Washing hands can help, and doctors can also prescribe medicine that can kill the worms.

Around raccoons

I don't remember eating those.

Raccoon roundworm is a parasite carried by raccoons that can infect humans and make them very sick. Cases are rare and are mainly found in children who play in dirt that's infected by raccoon poop. Proper hand washing, and avoiding raccoon waste, are good methods of preventing infection.

Beaver fever

Beaver fever is a stomach bug caused by a tiny parasite found in poop. It's normally passed on by drinking infected water. Symptoms of beaver fever include diarrhea, stomach pain, and burps that smell like eggs. It can be cured with antibiotics, but some people can recover without taking medicine.

Uninvited guest

When a man in India went to the hospital after suffering stomach pains for two months, the doctors discovered a giant tapeworm inside his gut. The tapeworm was removed through the man's mouth. The man must have accidentally eaten or drank something that had the eggs of the tapeworm in it. The worm measured a whopping 6.2 feet (1.88 meters), the same length as a tall man!

BUTT OF THE JOKE

The gluteus maximus, the name of the muscle in your bottom, is the largest and heaviest muscle in the body. Let's find out all about brilliant butts!

Nothing butt trouble

Have you ever wondered why we have butts at all? Researchers generally agree that our butts help keep us upright and give us balance when moving. You can, however, develop "dead butt syndrome," which happens if you sit down for a long time. To combat this, you should take regular breaks where you, and your butt, are more active.

R.I.P. BUTT

Bum note

"The Booty Drum" is a device that attaches to the butt of a dancer. The device contains a set of sensors that track the movement of the dancer's butt. The movements are used by a computer to create a finished music track.

Butt strength

As with other muscles, you can build a bigger, stronger butt through specific exercises. Squats, lunges, and weight lifting can all help to grow the butt muscles. Mr. Cherry, from Japan, holds a number of bizarre world records, including one for crushing walnuts with his butt.

Artist Richard Jackson created an exhibition of sculptures that squirted paint out of their butts and onto a wall.

MIND BOGGLING

The phrase "mind boggling" means something is startling or overwhelming. Here are some facts about the brain to stretch your mind!

Go put a coat on!

Ice shrink

After a group of scientists had spent 14 months in Antarctica, it was discovered that their brains had shrunk. Scans before and after the expedition showed that the areas responsible for memory, learning, and emotions had become smaller. The changes may have been caused by spending over a year in the same building, with the same people, looking at the same blank landscape.

Daydreamers

Researchers have found that people whose minds regularly wander score more highly in intelligence and creativity tests than those whose minds don't. So next time your teacher scolds you for daydreaming in class, you have the perfect excuse!

Brain pain

The brain itself can't feel pain since it has no pain receptors. Instead, we feel pain when nerve endings sense damage and relay signals to our brains. One pain tolerance test includes plunging your hand into ice-cold water to see how long it takes before it really starts to hurt.

Brain teaser

Here's a quick question. Shout out the answer!

Mary's mother has four children: April, May, June, and ...?

SHORTCUT

The answer is, of course, Mary!

If you said "July," however, your brain is trying to be extra efficient. Our brains look for shortcuts to save time and energy, but it doesn't always mean we are correct!

SKIN SPECIAL

Skin is an organ that covers our bodies and protects us. It helps control our temperature and helps us detect things like pain. The thinnest skin is found on the eyelids and the thickest is found on the palms of the hands and the soles of the feet.

It's a stretch

If we peeled our skin off and stretched it out, it would cover about 21 square feet (two square meters), which is about the size of a picnic blanket. The world record for "stretchiest skin" belongs to Garry Turner who can pull the skin from his neck completely over his jaw.

Skin slurpers

Creepy, crawly, and slimy, maggots may not be an obvious medical prescription. Maggot therapy, however, is a very real treatment used to help heal wounds in patients. The maggots are very effective in eating the dead skin and rotting flesh around a wound, leaving the healthy tissue to heal.

Blisters are pockets of fluid that appear between the top layers of the skin. They are mostly caused by friction, freezing, burning, or infection. Blisters often occur on the feet when the skin has been rubbed through walking, running, or trying to escape from a grumpy parent who is trying to get you to clean your room.

Shedding skin

While snakes and other creatures shed their skin in one shot, we shed ours constantly at a rate of more than 30,000 skin cells a minute! This may explain why some of the dust we find in our homes is made up of dead human skin.

Humans are gross.

BRAINIACS!

The brain is like a supercomputer, storing and processing loads of information from the world around us. And, like computers, sometimes they need a reboot! Check out these brain-busting facts!

Brain fart!

A "brain fart" is the term used to describe that moment of blankness we sometimes get when we forget the answers to simple questions, or even simple words. Brain farts tend to increase with age and common ones include trying to remember names, faces, and where we've left something.

Pardon me!

Brain freeze

If you dig into ice cream or an ice pop too fast, then you may experience brain freeze. It happens when something very cold hits the roof of your mouth and nerves are triggered to cause a headache. Brain freeze is the body's way of telling you to slow down, no matter how tasty that ice cream is!

Electric jello

The human brain feels like jello and weighs about 2.9 pounds (1.3 kilograms)—the same as a large pineapple! Your brain generates enough electricity to power a light bulb.

OUTRAGEOUS ORGANS

There are 78 organs in the human body, all of which work together to keep us fit and healthy. From the stomach to the spleen—our organs do a lot to keep us going! Let's find out about some of the more interesting jobs our organs get up to.

Spleen, clean machine

At around 5 inches (13 centimeters) long, the same length as a mango, the spleen filters our blood, cleaning out bacteria and viruses. It also recycles damaged blood cells. The Bajau people in southeast Asia have larger spleens. This makes more blood—that carries oxygen—helping them dive deeply to collect shellfish from the seafloor.

So many jobs

The liver is the second largest organ after the skin—it's about the size of a football. It keeps our bodies healthy by converting food into energy, removing harmful toxins from the blood, and fighting infections. The liver can grow back if it is damaged, meaning people can donate part of their liver to patients who need it, and both livers will grow back to normal size.

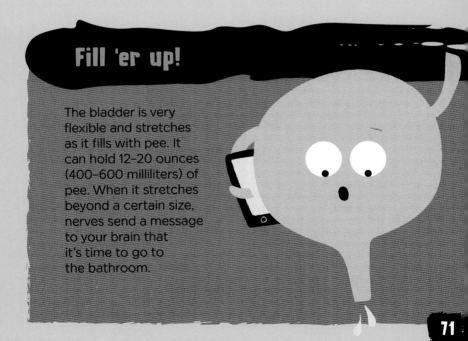

Fill 'er up!

The bladder is very flexible and stretches as it fills with pee. It can hold 12–20 ounces (400–600 milliliters) of pee. When it stretches beyond a certain size, nerves send a message to your brain that it's time to go to the bathroom.

HAIRY SCARY

Hair covers almost all parts of the human body. The hairless areas include the lips, the palms of our hands, and the soles of our feet. You have more than 100,000 hairs on your head and each individual hair grows for between two and six years.

We have about the same number of hairs on our bodies as a chimpanzee. Our hairs, however, are very tiny and not as visible.

Head scratchers

Head lice or nits are tiny insects that live in your hair and feed on your blood. They grab onto strands of hair using their sticky feet and are easily spread. Millions of people get them each year. It is not a sign of being dirty or unclean.

Hair grows from follicles in the skin, and the roots are the only living part of your hair. The hair we actually see is dead, that's why it doesn't hurt when you have your hair cut! (Unless you have a very bad barber.)

Hooray for hair!

Despite being pretty thin, hair is very stretchy and strong. A single hair can hold 0.2 pounds (100 grams), the same weight as a lemon, and a whole head of hair can support the weight of two elephants!

GROW UP!

From the terrible twos to our teenage years, our bodies and minds develop in a number of ways. Here, you can find out all about the changes that happen as we grow up!

Early riser

We are taller in the morning than we are during the rest of the day. This is because cartilage, the stuff that connects our bones, becomes compressed as we go about our day. We become about 0.4 inches (1 centimeter) taller after we've had a night's sleep.

Spot the difference

Most teens will experience acne, which comes in the form of pimples or zits. They are pus-filled bumps that appear on the skin, and happen when tiny holes called pores get clogged up with germs, oil, and dead skin. It is very common and a normal part of growing up.

My little boy!

When you haven't seen a relative for a long time, one of the first things they may mention is how much you've grown. This could also be due to the time of the year they last saw you, since children grow quicker in the spring!

Aches and pains

Throbbing or aching legs might not just be a sign that you've been doing too much dancing or sports. Growing pains are common among active children, between the ages of 3 and 12. Although painful, they are just signs that you are getting bigger and growing up.

OUCH!

Bumps, cuts, and scrapes—our bodies are used to some rough treatment. On these pages you can find out about all the things that make you say "ouch!"

Fall guy

The most common injury among children is falling. But as painful as falling is, it doesn't make it onto a list of the most painful conditions that humans experience. These include frozen shoulder, cracked ribs, and trigeminal neuralgia, which is said to feel like getting an electric shock to the face.

What a shiner!

When we bump ourselves we may find that bruises appear. Tiny blood vessels under the skin break and blood begins to leak out. Trapped under the skin with nowhere to go, purple or bluish marks appear and are tender to touch. The color of a bruise will change as the body repairs itself.

Snap!

Broken bones, also known as fractures, can happen when people fall or have accidents. It can be very painful, and the broken bone may look crooked. Doctors use X-rays to see how breaks need to be treated, and then use casts, made up of a bandage and a hard covering, to protect the bone as the body heals itself.

Didn't feel a thing

Congenital insensitivity to pain, or CIP, is a rare condition where people are unable to feel pain. While this may sound like a good thing, it can actually be difficult to live with, since people could get badly injured, yet have no idea.

Watch out!

SLEEP TIGHT

Sleep is an important function that allows our bodies and minds to recharge, heal, and store memories so that we are refreshed and ready for action when we wake up. The amount of sleep we need depends on our age, with children between the ages of 5 and 12 needing around 11 hours and a baby as much as 15!

Dream on

Dreams can be fun, scary, or just plain weird. Most people can remember parts of their dreams but as much as 95 percent of our dreams are forgotten shortly after we wake up. In an attempt to combat this, some people try to capture their dreams by writing in a "dream diary." Some of these have even ended up as published books!

Late night

Starting in December 1963, 17-year-old Randy Gardner stayed awake for 11 days in a row trying to beat the previous world record. After his record, Randy slept for 14 hours before getting up and going to school the next day. This can be dangerous and is not recommended!

Zzzzzzzz

Sleepwalkers do not always walk, some may also just sit up in bed. Although their eyes are usually open, sleepwalkers do not act the same as they would if they were awake. It can be confusing or scary for sleepwalkers if they are startled.

Loudest snore

Grandmother Jenny Chapman can drown out the sounds of a washing machine, tractor, and train. Her world-record-breaking snore was registered at over 111 decibels, which is the same as if a jumbo jet were flying over your house.

Zzzzzzzz

Can you keep it down?

OPEN WIDE

Teeth begin to develop before we are born, and start to come in when babies are about six to nine months old. By three years old, most children will have their full set of 20 baby teeth, which will eventually fall out to be replaced with 32 adult teeth.

Baby teeth

One in every 2,000 babies are born with at least one tooth already in their mouths. Sean Keaney from the UK made the news in 1990 when he was born with 12 teeth. To avoid problems with feeding, they were removed. His second set grew in a few years later.

Mighty molars

Tooth enamel is the hardest substance in the human body, but it can't heal itself like bones can. It is harder than steel, but more brittle, meaning it can be chipped by biting down on hard objects, or through accidents. Scientists are able to find out a lot of information about our ancestors by studying the teeth in ancient skeletons.

Tasty paste

Mint is the most common flavor of toothpaste, but there are a lot of others out there. These include cupcake, mint chocolate, pumpkin, bacon, and charcoal. It's also possible to start your day by brushing your teeth with octopus-flavored toothpaste.

If you brush your teeth for two minutes, twice a day, that means you brush your teeth for a total of 24 hours every year.

NASTY NAILS

Fingernails and toenails are made of keratin, which is the same material found in horse hooves and rhino horns. Our fingernails grow slowly at around 0.1 inches (2.5 millimeters) a month. Toenails grow even more slowly and losing one can mean waiting for a year and a half before it completely grows back.

Not such a fungi

Toenail fungus can cause the toenail to become yellow or brown, and a lot thicker than normal. Unlike other conditions, the fungus will rarely go away by itself and, if left untreated, may cause the nail to crumble and fall off.

Nail art

Getting your fingernails or toenails painted is a very popular thing to do, but some people have taken "nail art" to a whole new level. Rachel Betty Case is an artist that uses toenail clippings to create miniature skeletons of animals.

Nail chompers

Biting your nails is a common habit, but it can cause illness due to germs that are lurking under your nails. Even after washing your hands, bacteria, fungus, and yeast can all still be there, waiting to be popped into your mouth.

Longest nails

The world's longest fingernails on a single hand belonged to Shridhar Chillal, and measured a total of 358 inches (909.6 centimeters), about the same length as two cars! He only grew the nails on his left hand and kept his right hand trimmed, so he could still do his job as a photographer.

EAR ALL ABOUT IT!

Our ears are made up of three parts: the inner, middle, and outer ear. Ears collect sounds, which are then sent to the brain. Humans can hear a wide range of sounds but, weirdly, many children can't seem to hear their parents when they ask them to do chores!

Wax facts

Sticky, shiny, and stinky, ear wax has an important job in protecting our ears. It can help fight off infection and prevent unwanted objects from entering the ear canal. It is made up of dead skin cells, hair, and oil.

Cauliflower ears

Wrestlers can suffer from something called "cauliflower ear." During the rough and tumble of the match, the ears can end up being bumped and twisted out of shape, leaving them looking lumpy and swollen.

Open all hours

Parp!

We can hear even when we're asleep. Our ears continue to work as normal, but our brains filter out noises that may otherwise wake us up. Loud noises may still wake you up, such as a loud bang, or someone farting.

Roller-coaster ride

If you've ever felt sick on a roller-coaster, this is due to your inner ear. The inner ear contains fluid that sends information to our brains about movement and balance. When this fluid is sloshed around quickly your brain can get confused messages, meaning you might start to feel sick.

FESTERING FACTS

There are lots of gross and ghastly things going on around you. Here are some quick facts that are sure to make you go "Eww!"

Micro mites

Most people have tiny mites that live on their eyelashes. The microscopic creatures eat dead skin cells found on our eyelashes or eyelids.

Phone crawl

Scientists at the University of Arizona have found that your phone is home to 10 times more bacteria than your toilet seat!

Ugh, so gross.

Family Farts

People who live and eat together smell the same. That means your farts will smell similar to your family members' farts! Take a whiff and test it out.

Clean clothes

Our saliva contains an enzyme that breaks down our food. It is the same enzyme that is used in laundry detergent to clean stains off clothes! Enzymes are things that speed up chemical reactions.

OLD NEWS

Changes happen on both the inside and outside of our bodies as we age. Here are some of the things you can expect to happen when you get older!

Huge changes

As you get older, your ears and nose get bigger. One of the main reasons for this is because of gravity, which causes those features to sag.

Getting shorter

As we get older, our bones lose calcium, a mineral which is important for bone health, making them more fragile and likely to break. The bones in our spines get thinner and the squishy discs between them become smaller. This reduces our overall height so that by 70 years old, we may have lost of over 1 inch (2.5 centimeters) in height!

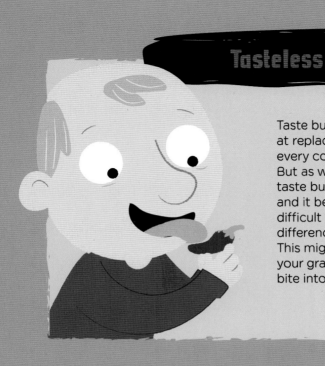

Taste buds are pretty good at replacing themselves every couple of weeks. But as we get older, our taste buds stop doing this, and it becomes more difficult to notice the difference between tastes. This might explain why your grandparents can bite into a hot chili pepper!

No sweat

Researchers have found that our sweat glands shrink as we age, so while you may be dripping with sweat after running around, you might find that your grandmother is barely breaking a sweat.

HORRID HANDS

Found at the end of our arms, hands allow us to perform a range of complex tasks such as grabbing, lifting, and writing. Most people have two hands and have five fingers on each. Without hands we wouldn't be able to poke, prod, pick our noses, or point to our favorite gross facts on this page!

Roman emperor Julius Caesar ordered the thumbs of captured warriors to be cut off so that they wouldn't be able to pick up weapons.

Handy Facts

Our hands are covered in bacteria. Research shows that bacteria can survive on hands for up to three hours, and that damp hands spread 1,000 times more germs than dry hands. Since 80 percent of illness-causing germs are spread by the hands, it is important to wash your hands regularly with soap and water.

Ouch!

Each year in the US, around 30,000 people are rushed to hospitals because they have accidentally amputated a finger. The two most common causes are related to power tools and doors.

Put your hands together

Antton Puonti won a national talent contest in Finland by using his hands to make fart noises. Puonti squeaked out a performance of John Lennon's song *Happy Xmas (War Is Over)* to scoop up the $35,000 prize.

COOL TRICKS

The human body is amazing. No need for cartwheels and somersaults here though, you can try these cool tricks from the comfort of the chair you're sitting in right now.

Look closely

Optical illusions happen when the messages between our brain and eyes get mixed up. Images that can be looked at one way can also be seen in another. One famous illusion, first seen in 1892, is pictured here. What do you see? A duck or a rabbit?

Strength test

Ever heard the phrase "didn't lift a finger"? It's usually about people who are lazy... but try this! Bend your middle finger and place the bent part onto a surface. Spread out the rest of your fingers so they're touching the surface too and then lift them one by one. You can lift your thumb, pinkie, and index finger but your ring finger suddenly becomes impossible to lift!

Impossible task?

Our bodies can do a range of incredible things, but even we have our limitations. Try touching your elbow. Easy? If you use an opposite hand to an opposite elbow it is. Now try touching your right elbow with your right hand. Impossible, right?

Brain training

Brain training is a set of activities designed to improve your brain's performance. Scientific evidence varies on how effective it can be but a lot of the activities are fun to do. Look at the objects below for 20 seconds and then cover them with your hand. How many can you remember?

GET ON YOUR NERVES

The nervous system controls everything we do, including thinking, moving, and breathing. It is made up of our brain, our spinal cord, and nerves that help take messages back and forth between the brain and the rest of our body. We have more than seven trillion nerves creating an estimated 90,000 miles (145,000 kilometers) of pathways. Sensational!

No choice

If we clap our hands or pick something up, we are thinking and choosing to do these actions. Part of our nervous system, however, is autonomic, which means we perform some actions without thinking about them. Autonomic actions include breathing, digestion, and drooling.

So annoying!

What gets on your nerves? This is a phrase that you may have heard your parents or friends say. But what is the answer? Scientists have investigated this by playing a range of sounds and asking people to rate which were most annoying. Some of the highest ranking annoying sounds were:

Snoring
Loud chewing
Car alarms
A knife scraped on a bottle

Pins and needles

Pins and needles is used to describe the tingling or prickly sensation we sometimes get in our hands, legs, and feet. It happens when the blood supply to our nerves is cut off, usually from sitting or sleeping on that part of our body.

BACK FOR MORE

Our spine is not one long bone but actually made up of 30 bones called vertebrae that allow us to bend, twist, and turn. The spine supports our weight and carries nerves that connect our brains to the rest of our body.

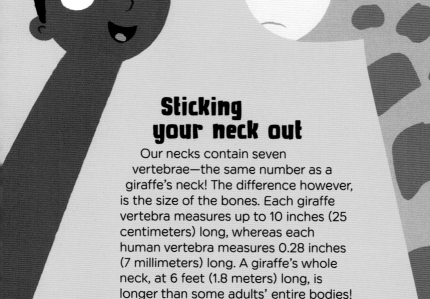

Sticking your neck out

Our necks contain seven vertebrae—the same number as a giraffe's neck! The difference however, is the size of the bones. Each giraffe vertebra measures up to 10 inches (25 centimeters) long, whereas each human vertebra measures 0.28 inches (7 millimeters) long. A giraffe's whole neck, at 6 feet (1.8 meters) long, is longer than some adults' entire bodies!

Bendy backs

Our spines are more flexible than you might think but some people have superflexible spines. Contortionists are particularly flexible and some can perform foot archery, holding a bow and arrow with their feet, before shooting over their heads at a target, all while in a handstand. Don't try that at home!

Out of this world

Astronauts who return from space missions find that they are taller than when they left. This is due to the lack of gravity in space that allows discs in the spinal column to expand. The effects do not last long, however, and they will quickly return to their normal size.

R.I.P.

Death is something that is permanent and will happen to all living things, including humans. Dead things do not eat, sleep, or breathe but it doesn't stop them from being gross!

Changing times

After death, the body goes through a whole process of decomposition. It may appear as if the hair and nails are growing, but actually, this effect is due to the skin drying out and shrinking.

Still got it

For up to three hours after death, human bodies have been known to continue burping and farting. Any air left in the body that is released may even make the vocal cords, vibrate causing the body to moan and groan.

Freezing to death

The practice of cryonics is when, before dying, people pay to have their remains frozen in special chambers, in the hope that they can be brought back to life in the future. The dead person's blood is replaced with special chemicals, which won't damage the cells like ice would.

And on that farm...

Some people decide to donate their bodies to "body farms," which are outdoor labs where scientists can study how bodies decompose in different situations. The results can help the police with crime investigations.

ICKY STICKY

Mucus is found in multiple areas of our bodies, including our mouth, lungs, stomach, and intestines. Snot is a form of mucus, but it isn't the only one. On this page, find out all about the icky, sticky stuff!

Thick and thin

Mucus can be runny or thick. Thick, jellolike mucus in the nose can be a sign that the air is very dry, or that you have a bacterial infection. If some people feel congested, they may choose to use a neti pot. It involves pouring a mixture of salt and water up one nostril and letting it flush through to the other, bringing mucus with it.

Man-eating fruit!

If you're looking to clear out mucus, then eating pineapple might be a solution. Enzymes in the juice have strong anti-inflammatory properties, which break down mucus and help some people cough it up more easily. Those very same enzymes that break down proteins, however, do the same to our mouths, which is why our tongues have that fizzy feeling after eating a lot of pineapple—in a way it's eating us back!

Sticky subject

Our guts are full of bacteria and we need to hang on to the good ones to make sure we stay healthy. Luckily, cells in our guts produce immunoglobulins, which cover the good bacteria and make them sticky. Scientists believe that these sticky bacteria are then held safely in the gut.

Let's stick around!

On the web

Fans of Spider-Man may be interested to know that scientists studied animals that climb to figure out how humans might be able to do the same. Sadly, the results may crush those dreams. To replicate how Spidey crawls we would need to be covered in sticky pads from our toes to the tops of our chests.

RELATIVELY SPEAKING

Genetics is the study of how we inherit features or characteristics from our parents. The DNA that's in our genes can also be used by scientists to study a whole range of living organisms and how they have evolved over time. Some of the studies link humans to some very unexpected things.

Chipper chimps

More than 98 percent of human DNA is shared with chimpanzees. They have facial expressions, can use tools, and even use plants as medicine for an upset stomach. Some have even learned sign language and have actually used it to communicate naughty words!

Cat person

If you like basking in the sun, drinking milk, or playing with balls of string, a study from 2007 may explain why. Scientists found that about 90 percent of our genes are shared with the domestic cat!

Hey, cousin!

Vegetable relations

It is not just animals that we share our DNA with. Scientists have found that we are related to a number of fruits and vegetables, including mushrooms and lettuce. Another study also suggests we share more than 40 percent of our DNA with a banana!

Elderly relative

Who is the oldest person in your family? Scientists have discovered the "oldest human ancestor." The 540-million-year old creature was discovered in central China and shows the earliest evolutionary steps to us becoming humans. It was about 0.04 inches (1 millimeter) in size and is thought to have lived between grains of sand on the seabed.

Hello, dear. Haven't you grown?

Gallstones and kidney stones come in a variety of shapes and colors and can be pretty painful, too! They are caused by a buildup of certain chemicals and minerals and can be as tiny as a grain of sand or as big as a golf ball.

Rock star

Vilas Ghuge has the honor of having had the world's largest kidney stone removed from his body in 2004. The stone measured a whopping 5 inches (13 centimeters), which is as long as a ballpoint pen. It was removed from Ghuge's kidney, and was bigger than the kidney itself.

Famous writer Samuel Pepys kept one of his kidney stones as a memento.

You rock

Gallstones are produced in the gallbladder and form hard lumps that are shaped like pebbles. Kidney stones are produced in the kidneys and are more crystal-like in appearance. Although some stones may need to be removed by doctors, some people will pass smaller gallstones in their poop, and kidney stones in their pee. Don Winfield from Canada holds the record for most stones passed in pee, with more than 6,500 making their way out over a period of 22 years!.

Stone age

In 2019, as part of an exhibition at the Science Museum in London, there was a gallstone and kidney stone museum where visitors could marvel at a range of stones extracted from patients.

LOUSY LEFTOVERS

Humans have evolved over thousands of years. Over that time, parts of our body that were once useful are no longer needed. Find out all about our lousy leftovers and extinct structures!

Wisdom teeth

Due to a diet of tough roots and uncooked meat, our ancestors had a real need for the wisdom teeth at the back of our mouths. Nowadays we don't need them because our jaws are smaller, so some people have them removed. Keeping them does add time to your toothbrushing routine!

Appendix

The appendix is a small, thin tube that is found in the lower stomach. While some scientists say it is helpful for bacteria in our gut, problems with the appendix can cause serious health issues. It is perfectly possible to have it removed and not notice any difference.

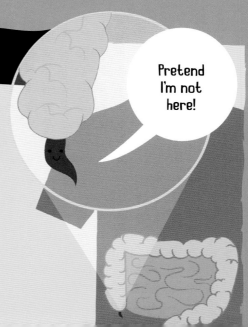

Pretend I'm not here!

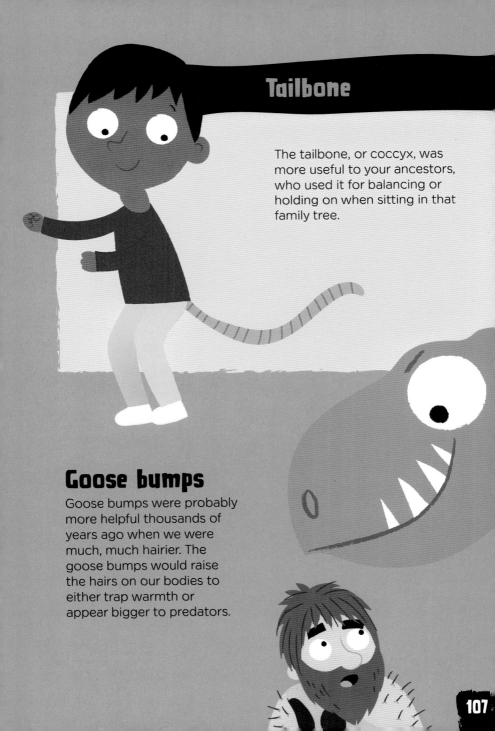

Tailbone

The tailbone, or coccyx, was more useful to your ancestors, who used it for balancing or holding on when sitting in that family tree.

Goose bumps

Goose bumps were probably more helpful thousands of years ago when we were much, much hairier. The goose bumps would raise the hairs on our bodies to either trap warmth or appear bigger to predators.

BACK TO STOOL

Poop can be runny, lumpy, or smooth, and can say a lot about your health. In the late 1990s, experts at the Bristol Royal Infirmary in the UK developed a chart to describe all the different types of poop.

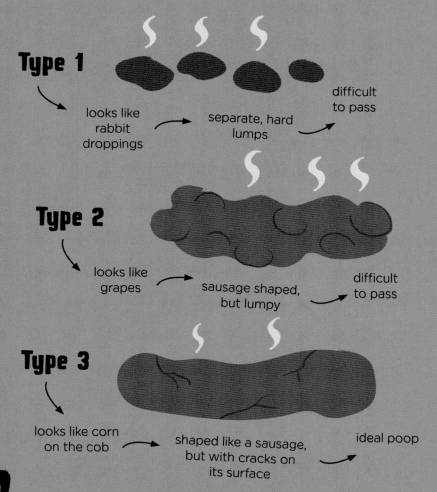

Type 1

looks like rabbit droppings → separate, hard lumps → difficult to pass

Type 2

looks like grapes → sausage shaped, but lumpy → difficult to pass

Type 3

looks like corn on the cob → shaped like a sausage, but with cracks on its surface → ideal poop

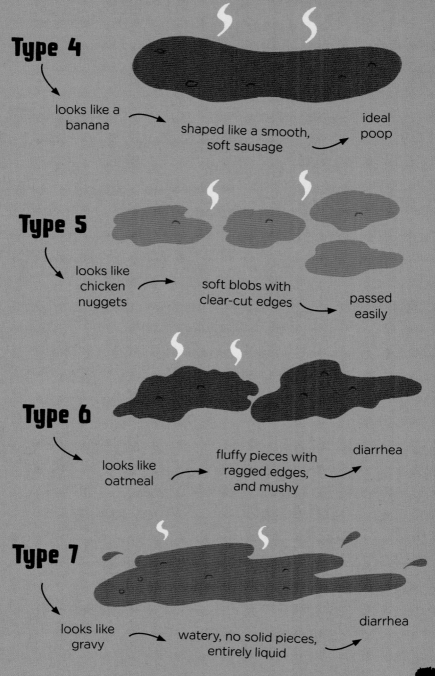

Type 4

looks like a banana → shaped like a smooth, soft sausage → ideal poop

Type 5

looks like chicken nuggets → soft blobs with clear-cut edges → passed easily

Type 6

looks like oatmeal → fluffy pieces with ragged edges, and mushy → diarrhea

Type 7

looks like gravy → watery, no solid pieces, entirely liquid → diarrhea

WHERE DO THEY GO?

Use your finger to match the body parts to their location in the illustration.

1 **Kidney**

2 **Liver**

3 **Stomach**

4 **Heart**

5 **Brain**

6 **Lung**

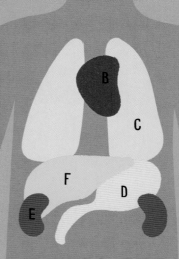

Can you match the names of the organs to their short descriptions? Use your finger.

MATCH THE ORGANS

1. **Bladder**
2. **Stomach**
3. **Lungs**
4. **Heart**
5. **Brain**
6. **Skin**

A I've got you covered.

B I fill with pee.

C You need me to breathe.

D I pump blood around your whole body.

E I break down your food.

F I am your control center.

TRUE OR FALSE?

1. The brain can't feel pain.

2. Our nails keep growing after we die.

3. We fart enough gas every day to fill up a balloon.

4. We are taller in the morning than we are at the end of the day.

5. The world's longest mustache is 131 feet (40 meters) long.

Can you find a way through the brain maze? Use your finger to follow the path to the finish.

BRAIN MAZE

Start

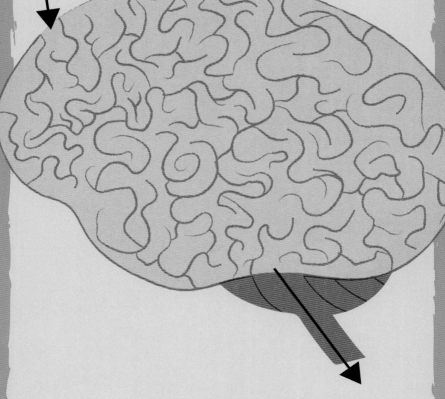

Finish

OPTICAL ILLUSIONS

Look carefully at these optical illusions. What can you see?

1 Which squares are bigger—the black or white ones?

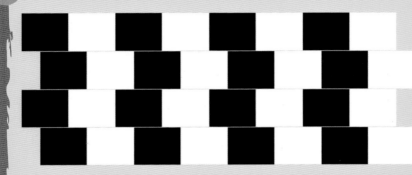

2 Which arc is bigger?

3   Is the center circle bigger in picture A or B?

A

B

4   Where does this begin and end?

5   Which character is taller?

A

B

C

REACTION TIME

Read the first part of each story below and then point to the face that would best describe your reaction. Then read the second part. Do you pick a different face when you've read the second part?

You dropped your dinner on the floor...

Your dinner was cold cabbage and fried boogers.

It's your birthday party...

Someone has eaten the last piece of cake, which you wanted.

You have a brand-new pair of sneakers...

But you've just stepped in dog poop.

You have been given extra homework

To test a new computer game.

You have just won lots of money in a competition...

The "World's Stinkiest Fart" Competition.

Happy

Disgusted

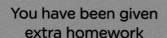

Sad

Angry

Excited

Now try making up some of your own stories and playing with a friend!

SPOT THE DIFFERENCE

Can you spot the 10 differences between these pictures? Use your finger to point them out!

You've read the
book, now let's see
what gross, ghastly,
and awesome facts
you learned!

END
OF BOOK
QUIZ!

1 Over our lifetimes, how much
saliva do we produce?
   A 2 bathtubs
   B 100 bathtubs
   C 27 bathtubs
   D 50 bathtubs

2 How many bones (vetebrae) does
your spine have?
   A 20
   B 5
   C 60
   D 30

3 Which of these gets bigger in
old age?
   A Your ears
   B Your tongue
   C Your bottom
   D Your brain

4 Which of these is a real disease?
   A Caterpillar cough
   B Beaver fever
   C Salamander syndrome
   D Donkey disease

5 What food do our brains
feel like?
   A Peanut butter
   B Ice cream
   C Jello
   D Cake

PIT STOP!

Many teenagers and adults wear deodorants to make them smell good. They come in a variety of fragrances and they even include smells such as pizza, bacon, and coffee.

Imagine you are designing a new deodorant spray.

Grab a piece of paper and create an ad to sell your new product.

What would you call it?

What scent would it have?

Think of a cool name, with a catchy slogan.

Don't forget to design the packaging!

ANSWERS

Where do they go?

1=E, 2=F, 3=D, 4=B, 5=A, 6=C

Match the organs

1=B, 2=E, 3=C, 4=D, 5=F, 6=A

True or false?

1 = TRUE! The brain has no pain receptors.

2= FALSE! It may look like they're growing but the skin is actually shrinking around them.

3 = TRUE! On average, we fart 14 times a day.

4 = TRUE! The cartilage in our spine becomes compressed during the day but it returns to normal when we sleep.

5 = FALSE! It is 13 feet (4 meters) long.

Brain maze

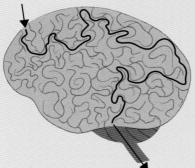

Optical illusions

1 = The are all the same!

2 = They are both the same!

3 = They are both the same!

4 = There is no beginning or end.

5 = They are all the same!

Spot the difference

End of book quiz!

1 = D, 50 bathtubs

2 = D, 30

3 = A, Your ears

4 = B, Beaver fever

5 = C, Jello

GLOSSARY

acid
A substance that dissolves things

amputate
When part of a person's body has been cut off for medical reasons

antibiotic
A medicine that is used to fight infections caused by bacteria

bacteria
Tiny living things that can live in and on our bodies. Some bacteria can be harmful

cartilage
Tough and flexible tissue that mostly helps connect bones

cells
Tiny pieces of living matter that make up the human body

chemicals
Substance that is made when two or more substances react

cryonics
Way of preserving dead human bodies at very cold temperatures

decibels
Units used to measure sound levels

decomposition
Process that happens to living things when they die, also known as rotting

dehydrated
When the body doesn't have enough water to function properly

DNA
Chemical that stores all the information about how our bodies will grow and work

enzyme
A substance that controls the speed of biochemical reactions

evolutionary
Process of how living things have developed over time

fossil
Remains of a prehistoric animal or plant

fractures
Broken bones

germs
Bacteria or viruses

glands
Parts of the body that make different chemicals

infection
When viruses or bacteria enter the body and make you sick

infectious
When something spreads easily

keratin
A material that forms our nails and hair

mucus
Thick, slimy fluid

nerve
Fiber that carries messages to the brain

nutrients
Chemicals that make up food, which the body needs for growth and repair

oxygen
Gas that we need to breathe to stay alive

plasma
A yellow liquid that is part of the blood

platelets
Tiny cells that help your blood to clot

receptor
Part of the body that picks up information

tissue
Group of cells that look and act the same

toxins
Dangerous chemicals

urine
Scientific name for pee

virus
Tiny thing from outside the body that invades cells

INDEX